Feeling

Julie Haydon

Contents

Rigby®

A Harcourt Achieve Imprint

www.Rigby.com
1-800-531-5015

Skin

You have skin on your body.
Skin helps the inside
of your body to stay safe.

Feeling

You feel with your skin, too.

You can feel things.

You can feel plants
and animals and people.

Hard or Soft

You can feel things
that are hard or soft.

A rock feels hard.
Yarn feels soft.

Wet or Dry

You can feel things
that are wet or dry.

Water feels wet.
A towel feels dry.

Hot or Cold

You can feel things that are hot or cold.

This drink feels hot.
Ice cream feels cold.

Feeling Hot or Cold

Your body can feel hot or cold.

This girl was feeling hot.
She had a cold drink.
Now she does not feel hot.

This boy was feeling cold.

He put on warm clothes.

Now he does not feel cold.

Lots of Things

You can feel many things at one time.

This girl can feel:
- the wind in her hair
- the clothes on her body
- the ball in her hands
- the sand under her feet

Things That Move

You can feel things that move.

This dog is moving. The boy can feel that the dog is moving.

This bike is moving.

The girl can feel

that the bike is moving.

Things That Hurt

Some things do not feel good.

Some things can hurt you.

Stay away from things
that can hurt you.

Glossary

towel

yarn